VOLCANO

Claire Saxby · Jess Racklyeft

ALLEN&UNWIN
SYDNEY · MELBOURNE · AUCKLAND · LONDON

Deep in the ocean,

far beyond the reach of even the brightest sun,

the earth quakes.

Hagfish scatter and snailfish flutter.

Lava pillows flash and fade,

rumple the seabed as a new volcano births a new mountain.

As the mountain pushes up, the seabed around it cracks.
Cold sea water seeps through to where magma roils.
Needles of scorching water pierce the ocean floor.

Where hot meets cold, a chimney forms.

As the chimney grows,

it becomes home to tiny bacteria afloat in the currents.

Tube worm larvae anchor, wave red feather-gills.

Pale-shell shrimp scuttle.

Ghostly fish nibble.

Here begins a colony of unexpected creatures.

The seabed rumbles and the volcano erupts again.
The vent that fed the chimney closes.
Bacteria, tube worms and crabs drift away.

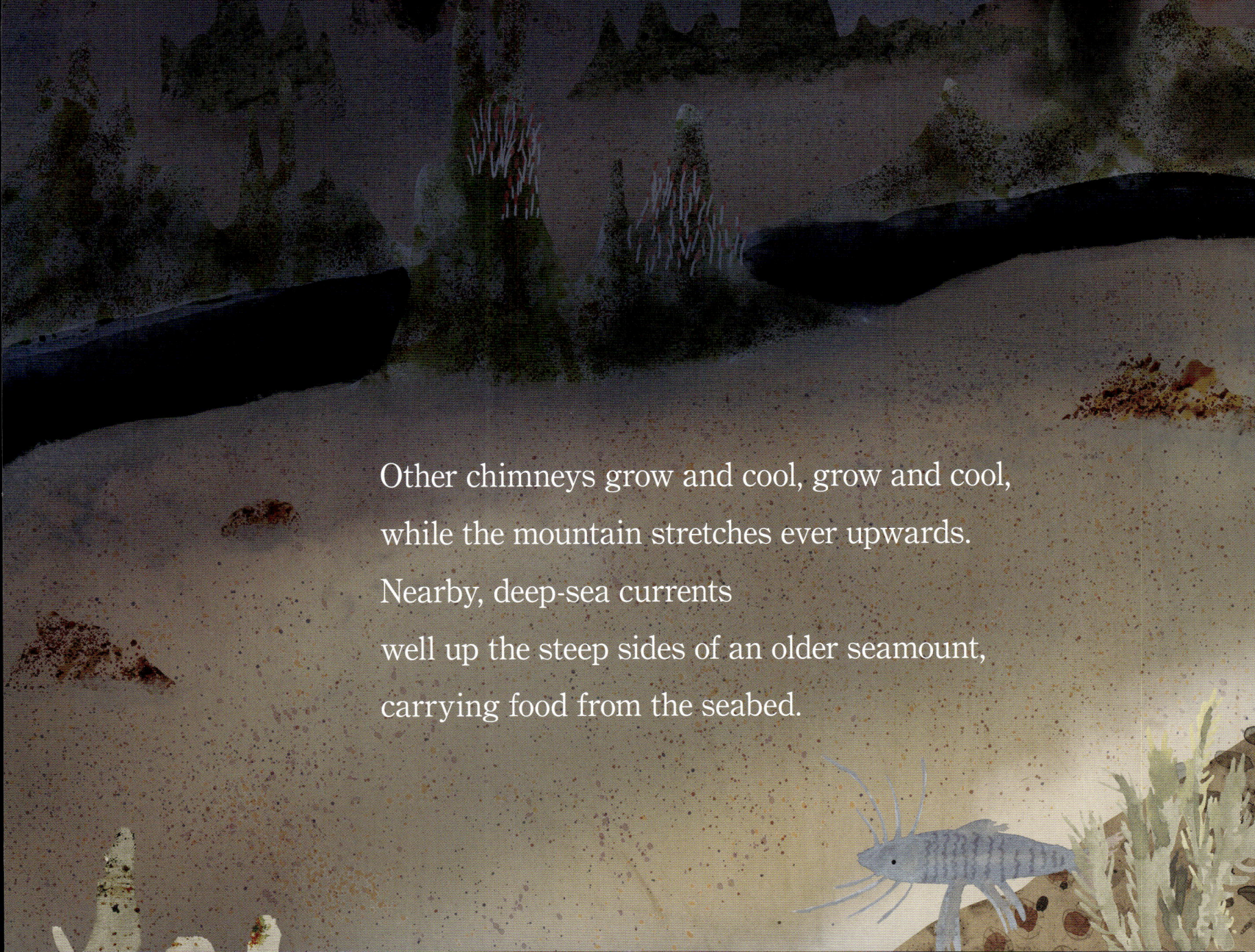

Other chimneys grow and cool, grow and cool,

while the mountain stretches ever upwards.

Nearby, deep-sea currents

well up the steep sides of an older seamount,

carrying food from the seabed.

Phytoplankton feed and bloom. Feathery corals sprout.

Mussels and limpets take hold. Sponges swell.

Red-legged crabs nibble and scrabble. Young redfish circle.

Tuna arrive, feed and swim on.

Sea turtles pause.

Sharks and whales pass by on their ocean journeys.

The volcano erupts again and again,

each explosion more fractious.

The mountain climbs until it is within reach of the sky.

A rumble becomes a roar and the sea boils.

Eventually, the lava slows.
Steam evaporates.
Clouds clear and waves calm.
The earth becomes still.

The exploding volcano breaches.
Lava fireworks the sky.
Black smoke belches and bulges.
Rocks pepper the jostling waves.

The volcano that built
an underwater mountain,
that built an island,
is finally silent.

Rains fall and winds blow.
The island cools
and the lava cracks.
Waves wash the shore.

On land and in the water, new life begins.

Seeds sprout and stretch.

Branches spread wide and tall.

Seagulls hover and fingerlings dart.

Eggs hatch.

Back on the seabed, the earth quakes.

Pillows of lava ooze and are quenched.

The seabed changes as a new volcano births a new mountain.